BLOOD RED

A Memoir of Reflection on Family Ties and Relationships

Dr. Carol Lemley Montgomery

Editorial Contributions by
Susan E. Reynolds, Ph.D.
Ana Yousuf-Starns, Ph.D.

Copyright © 2023 Dr. Carol Lemley Montgomery

All rights reserved. No part of this book may be reproduced or transmitted in any form or by any means, electronic or mechanical, including photocopying, recording, or by any information storage and retrieval system, without permission in writing from the copyright Author.

This book was printed in the United States of America.

CONTENTS

Preface 1

Memoir 5

Afterword 75

Life Through Memories 81

A Life Dedicated to Equality, Education, and Empowerment 83

About the Author 87

PREFACE

The men came up from the mine which had been tunneled deep in Red Mountain and they then entered the commissary store. On their heads they wore their miner's caps with the carbide lamp on the front so light could shine where each man turned his head, shine on the seam of iron ore, leaving him free handed to do his work. They came into the commissary where they came to buy their bottled drinks and snacks. As they walked across the wood floors that creaked against their steel-toed boots, where I could see the red iron ore dust on their hands and faces.

I was small, a child allowed to roam about my father's work place, and had seen these men, knew what work they were taking a break from and I always noticed them. I saw them in the context of the world of my childhood where the color line, the ruling principle of racial differences between black and white was always present, always defining each person. These men stood aside from that color line because their skin seemed neither black nor white, but the temporary color of the work of mining iron ore, blood red: blood red dust of

Red Mountain's precious ore needed for the constant production of steel colored their hands and faces and we were briefly part of the same world there in the company store.

> Hematite: one of Earth's most abundant minerals, an iron oxide, found throughout the world and is an ore of iron. Hematite is a primary mineral on Earth and on planet Mars. The name hematite comes from the Greek word "haimatitis" which means "blood-red."
>
> Hematite is blood red in color when crushed finely and mixed with a liquid, was used as a dye by people where ever the ore was found. Paints and dyes made from hematite judged to be more than 40,000 years old have been found. Hematite can stain what it touches.

Memory can keep a mental image that is fragile but not static: over time memory can add and remove details of the image kept in mind, and if the memory was made in childhood, the images are out of proportion for an adult.

What I see in my mind's eye when I remember the commissary at Wenona looks like this: walking in the front door, the area which held the cold cases, the meat cooler and ice cream freezer, lay to the right. I was usually told by my dad to go in there and get an ice cream cone for myself as soon as I got entered the commissary. I didn't have to pay for it, and never knew if he came back later to pay or if free ice cream was a fringe benefit for the boss's daughter.

To the left of the front door was the dry goods department where some of the items for sale were clothes and toys, an area where I would inevitably spend time looking at the little family of mannequins. There was a life-sized male clothing model, a model woman and a little girl. Depending on the season they would be dressed in whatever was appropriate to demonstrate new clothing items in the store. The little girl mannequin was always in a dress, black or white patent leather shoes and socks, but no underwear. I know this because as soon as I walked into the clothing section, I made a bee line for that dress model to see if they had put any underwear on her.

Back in the front of the store, between the dry goods and cold counters, directly in line with the front door was the shoe department. Chairs were lined up along the wall that shielded the boxes of shoes from sight. Boxed shoes were shelved behind the wall, so if you walked behind it, the shelves created narrow walk spaces, a maze for hiding from my little brother. Overhead on the half floor above was the office for the entire store and where the clerical work was done. This area was off limits for us children. I cannot recall ever being allowed to walk up the staircase to the office even though I was free to range everywhere else in the store.

Behind the shoe section was the grocery department which was my dad's territory, where he was in charge. The grocery department sold the usual groceries, canned goods, plus sacks of flour stacked high, and the more unusual item of baby chicks in an incubator. There was a little cubby hole of a space back there, with a table and heavy wooden chairs where employees could take a break, have their lunch, it was another place where I liked to hang out, listening to the people who worked there talking and laughing. I suppose they had worked together for a long enough time to have that relaxed "work friendship" that develops, but I saw them as my dad's special friends. The days of running around and hiding from my brother did come to an end as soon as I was old enough to stock canned goods. The job I usually was given was to open a box of cans and stamp the price on each can then stock the cans on the shelves. Not much could go wrong doing that, and it kept me out of their way. I saw it as a very important job.

As I said, my father, Ed Lemley, was the grocery department manager of the company store, the Wenona commissary which was a part of the mining camp in Wenona, Jefferson County, Alabama that was owned by US Steel. The company store was one of the services available for miners and their families along with a dental clinic, the medical dispensary, and company houses. Although my family didn't live in the camp we did go to the dispensary where Dr. Clyde Garmon treated us, and we did get some of our groceries and clothes from the company store, so while I was in the store tagging along with my daddy, my life briefly overlapped with those of the miners, but when we went home it was to our life in West End, a suburb of Birmingham, Alabama and the blood red men went home to their company houses.

West End was one of the first residential areas that grew up somewhat removed from the original center of the scrappy, dirty, and loud boom town of Birmingham, whose founding date was 1871 and West End's development was about three decades later. West End was essentially a working-class residential area where the majority of the people living there were White and rented their houses, or roomed as boarders with families. They worked in the foundries, blast furnaces, mines, railroads, and saloons of the rough new town of Birmingham. West End's incorporation as a separate town lasted for about five years, from 1905 to 1910 when it was brought into the city limits of Birmingham along with some of the other little outlying communities There were also a couple of more affluent housing areas on the outskirts of the city, but they were smaller and not filled with the men and women who made up the manual labor force needed to create the great wealth that poured out of Birmingham, and out of the state.

The story, embellished I think, of how Birmingham came to be, and be called the Magic City and rivaled Pittsburg in its greatness as an industrial giant has been told and told and written about but I want to remember where I grew up from my birth on 25 April, 1943 to the time I left West End, and Alabama, in May, 1961. When I think of West End, I remember my house, my home, the neighborhood, all the people and events that created a life, the context for me to grow up feeling part of a vibrant living community. We lived in my grandmother's house, five adults, three children and a variety of animals in the back yard. There was a separation between where the humans lived and where the animals lived, with none of the animals ever entering the house. My father and my uncle had hunting dogs and the dogs lived in their fenced yard. When we did get a dog to be a pet it was a collie, but he never was allowed inside either. Rocky, what my sister named him, had been given to us by Dr. Garmon in Wenonah. I don't know if Rocky was given specifically to my sister, but my memory is that she named him and seemed to have been the one who took care of him. But then, my sister was five years older and I was in awe of all she did and said and was, in that way that a younger sibling is of the magical older one. She called me "Tag-along Tacky" in that unmagical way of older sisters who are stuck with minding the younger one till the adults came home from work.

Along with the dogs' yard was another space for the chickens where the chicken house was, where the chickens went to roost at night. The chickens spent days roaming freely in the back yard, sometimes roosting in the Mimosa tree. Our chickens were the variety Bantam, or Banties in our lingo. They are smaller than most other varieties and produce smaller eggs as well. The Bantam rooster had been given the name of "Sleep-in-the-tree" by my five-year-old brother, and the rooster did sleep in the Mimosa tree as often as he could get free of the hens and out of the henhouse in the chicken yard. There was a coal pile in one corner of the chicken yard for the coal that fired the furnace which heated our house. Chickens roamed about the yard, pecking and cackling at me when I had to enter the yard with the coal scuttle in hand to pick up coal and take back inside for the furnace. I was terrified of those chickens, certain that they were going to fly at me and peck me every time I went in their yard. Sometimes I carried a broom or rake along just in case I had to defend myself against a vicious chicken attack. And because there were chickens there were also large snakes we knew as Black Racers which we often saw slithering quickly across the yard. Oddly, I had no fear of the snakes, only the chickens.

The chickens weren't the only ones who liked to spend time in the Mimosa tree. It also served as a special gathering place for my sister and I and our neighborhood friends. My sister, being older and naturally in charge, had assigned seating spots on the broad branches of the tree to each of us. Our chief problem with sitting in that tree was the ants. We had other spots around our yard and the garages where we could meet and hide out from the grownups, but the Mimosa was in full view from the house so we didn't use it when we had high level kid stuff to discuss.

Our back yard was not large, but it held so much life, so many activities from the daily mundane to the once-a-year celebrations and barbeques, and ice cream made from a hand cranked White Mountain ice cream freezer, you know the kind, a wooden bucket with a locking device on top and a crank that turned the dasher inside the container where the ice cream was being made. The barbeque pit was also in the backyard where my dad and uncle practiced the ritual of slow cooking a large Boston butt into the most delicious food possible. The back yard was more private than the front yard, which was necessary for the men needed to keep up their barbequing strength with enough beer to make it less like work. We lived in a modest world of Protestant virtues and abstinence was expected of the men but they did not follow those expectations.

The front yard opened on to the entire neighborhood, and was the where we spent a lot of time in the summer with neighbors. It was the best spot for summer night time star gazing. The front yard was where the older folk sat at night after turning out the lights and the floor fans turned on to allow the house to cool down in the summer heat. No one had air conditioners, we all relied on open windows, front porches and fans. The back yard was a little more private, serving our family in a variety of ways, privacy, kid's playground, coal storage, and animal enclosures. At various times we had a male turkey and for a while, ducks. I have no idea where the turkey came from, probably something my uncle, the man I called "Papa" had gotten. He was my uncle because he was married to my mother's sister Alvice. We never called her by her given name; she was always Sissy to us. Her husband was named Harold F. Parler and called by all who knew him "Parler" except for the children. We called him Papa. He was a delight, a treasure, a funny and loving man who made me feel like the most special and beautiful child in the world. He gave me the only nickname I have ever had: Doodlebug – but in his South Carolina accent it came out "Du-duh-bug." His family had migrated from the north to South Carolina generations ago, carrying their French heritage and manner of speaking with them. When Papa told a joke, which was often, he would so amuse himself that he started laughing, dropping back into that Cajun accent, and sometimes I could barely understand him.

I understood how much he loved me. He was a butcher by trade and owned a small meat and grocery market, Parler's New Market, in West End. The glass-front cold case where the meat was displayed ran across most of the back of the store, with a shelf on the outside where bread was stacked, Along the right side of the room was the counter and cash register where customers would place their items to be rung up and bagged. When I was in his store, he liked to put me up on the counter near the cash register and proudly tell everyone that I was so beautiful that when I grew up, I was going to go to California and become famous, and make them all rich. "This is Duduhbug" he would say and I beamed. I basked in that love. He had a pay phone in the store that he would use to signal someone at home that he needed to talk to one of us. Instead of spending the dime that it cost to make a call, he would call home, let it ring once and hang up. We all knew that meant call the store and see what he wanted. It seems funny to me now to think about that, and wonder if it was a habit shaped by the experience of living through the Depression, or was he just that frugal that every dime counted? We were not poor, certainly always had enough of what was necessary, but he saved a dime. He also saved the old silver dollars that he received in the store. He and my aunt Sissy kept those silver dollars in a special bag and she would let me take them out and count them.

Papa's mother came to visit our house in West End, perhaps more than once but I remember one time only. She did something that fascinated me, that I had never seen anyone do before and really never have since then: she had a small cup, oval in shape and stood on a tiny pedestal, which she used to wash out her eyes. After her visit was over and she returned to her home in South Carolina I found that she had left the little cup in the medicine cabinet in the bathroom. There is one other small memory I have about that visit, one that is hard to even explain but I will tell it. The laundry hamper stood against the wall, just to the right of the toilet. The hamper was made of some sort of plastic, a soft finish, soft enough to be scratched with a sharp object. For some reason I chose to scratch words on the top of the hamper where anyone could see them and they were scatological words. My mother was very angry with me because a visitor was coming to stay in our house and there it was, on the hamper, "do-do." My poor mother, her child was clearly going to be an embarrassment for her for the rest of her life. There was no option such as the guest using the other bathroom because there was only one, for 5 adults and 3 children and I had decorated it with a word that embarrassed her.

Few middle-class families today would want to have to share just one bathroom in a house of 5 adults and 3 children, but we did. The bathroom, as was typical for the time the house was built in the late 1930s, lacked a shower and had a claw-foot bath tub. My sister-in-law told me a story about how my aunt, uncle, and grandmother bought the house during the Depression, making a commitment to pay the (now) insignificant amount of mortgage payments of about twenty-nine dollars a month, but an amount that was frighteningly large to them. By the time I was born there were three employed adults, Daddy, Papa, and Sissy (with my mother working only later) there to make sure the mortgage was being paid. My grandmother had a tiny income from being the widow of a man having been an employee with the railroad, Louisville & Nashville, or L&N as we knew it, so she had a bit of income of her own.

Being the widow of a man once employed by L&N also gave her free travel on the L&N passenger trains that once passed through our city of Birmingham. I traveled with her on the passenger train named the Humming Bird to visit her youngest sister Annie Hardenburg in Pascagoula, Mississippi. The Humming Bird was one of L&N's premier passenger trains which ran for thirty years beginning in 1939. It passed through Birmingham, Alabama, going on through coastal Mississippi to New Orleans, Louisiana. Initially the rail service on the Humming Bird originated in Cincinnati, Ohio running through Birmingham daily to its destination of New Orleans, but it's point of origin soon was changed to Chicago, Illinois. I never knew, or cared, where it started out, I only cared that I was going on the delicious adventure to visit my cousins in Mississippi with my grandmother. I continued to see those cousins for a few visits back and forth until we drifted away from that family connection as teenagers. However, before that slow drift away from my blood kin took place, we had fun together.

On one of the visits with my Mississippi cousins we went to the lake house that was owned by the company where my cousins' dad worked, International Paper. The company owned a two-story lake house for the use of some of the employees. I remember the visit especially because my cousin Forrest, 2 years older than I pushed me off the boat dock into the lake. He was the eldest of three children in that family, his sister Ann who was my age, and their little brother Phillips. Both of those dear boys died too young in their adult lives as men, but I still remember them with real affection. My relationship with my girl cousin was somewhat problematic, not because she was a problem but because her grandmother talked about her as if she were the heir to a throne. She took, and excelled according to her grandmother, piano lessons: I played nothing more than sand lot baseball in the neighborhood, she was so neat and tidy with her clothes that she changed immediately from her school dress to play clothing as soon as she arrived home from school: I came home from school late and muddy and barefoot from having gone the long way home so I could walk through the mud puddle that we played in near our house. She might have spoken French too for all I knew, but this was all when we were seven, eight, ten years old and I was jealous of her – and her grandmother was proud of her. I can see that now, but not then. All I saw was that I was a messy, unaccomplished "tomboy" of a girl who liked to climb trees and play softball in the vacant lot next door to our house. Thanks to my dad and my Papa, I knew how to seine minnows for fishing bait, how to aim and shoot a .22 squirrel rifle, how to skin the squirrels that they brought home from their hunting, how to churn milk to butter because we got fresh unpasteurized milk from a man who had cows, and how to tell a harmless black racer snake from the venomous snakes we might see in the woods. I can see now I was learning some useful life skills, although I didn't see it then.

Most of Ann's visits to me were to my grandmother's house, which was the house where I lived from the day my mother and father brought me home from the hospital and where I lived until I was 10. I was born on Easter, a very late day for Easter, at Lloyd Noland Hospital in 1943. That hospital was a part of the medical care available to the employees of United States Steel's mining and steel producing industry that made Birmingham. Lloyd Noland was the official name of the hospital, but none of us ever called it anything but "TCI" hospital, for the Tennessee Coal and Iron Company that had once owned the blood red ore and black coal mines that fed the huge furnaces of Jefferson County. My mother told me that I was born during what was called a black out, the attempt to lessen the amount of light that could be seen from the air by enemy airplanes, and while I have never heard that Birmingham actually was a target during World War II, it could have been so because of the heavy industrial war production taking place there. I was born in a steel town during a war, and taken home to live in a small house with a big family and good life. We lived in that house until I was ten years old, and most likely moved then only for my mother's sake, because my dad liked being in the midst of a large family.

When we did move it was only 3 blocks away but it was far enough away for my mother to finally be the adult woman in a house that did not also hold her mother, older sister, brother-in-law, husband, and three children. Living there with four other adults, all of whom were older than she, could not have been easy for her and I know that both my aunt and uncle would interfere when she tried to assert her authority over her children and apply some old-style discipline. My mother's choice of discipline was the infamous switch on bare legs, with which I had a lot of experience since I was a "headstrong" child. However, since my aunt and uncle both worked away from the house, until my mother also went to work too, she was free of their interference to do what she thought we needed. My uncle was especially tenderhearted and I do remember him saying "Now Ma'Hanks you don't need to spank that boy." Her name was Mary Frances, but in his South Carolinian drawl, it came out Ma'Hanks. We children - Jane, Eddie, and I, Carol, grew up with a lot of adults to give us the basics required for a good life.

My memories of childhood are still vivid and real.

Part of what made it a good life was the nature of my neighborhood and the freedom we had to roam within it. We were naturally what is now called "free range" children, but all children are supposed to be free to explore and investigate what catches their interests and stirs curiosity in their minds. How can children develop any creativity or learn to identify what calls to them to become without time and space to be self-directed in how they begin to shape their path in life? Maybe we were close to danger at times, but if we were, I didn't sense it. The two worse injuries I had as a child happened in the back yard. One injury was when I was about eight years old. A glass drink bottle had been broken in the yard and the base was hidden in the grass. The base had a large shard and I ran across it. It severed the tendon to a toe and hurt a lot. And once when much younger – perhaps three

– I was burned by the boiling water being used by my mother and aunt as they killed and cleaned chickens for a meal. I was burned because the laces of my high-top shoes were tied in knots in an effort to keep me from going barefoot and the hot leather increased the damage to my foot. I remember being taken to the medical clinic near the commissary store and being treated for a large blister on the top of my left ankle. It did not deter me from going barefoot.

My sister and I spent as much time outside of our house, away from adults and on our own as we could. We were hardly being neglected, we had boundaries of how far we were supposed to go, but of course we often overstepped the boundaries, going farther afield than what we knew were the limits. In Summer we went outside at night as soon as our supper (and yes in the South the last meal of the day is a supper) was done. We called it playing out – and we stayed outside until the street lights came on and the first mother called her child's name. This was the dread signal that meant a sudden awareness among all the other mothers that it was time for us to leave the street and come inside. When we played out at night, we had a large repertoire of games of chase and hide and seek. We had games where we ran at each other to see whose line of kids could hold up against the runner, but before any game could get started, we had to pick who was to be the first "It". To pick an It there had to be a "king-counter-out" person, a ``role usually taken by the oldest kid, someone's bossy older sister. Our typical way of choosing It was to put up two fists, while Miss Bossy Pants conducted the "one potato, two potato" ritual that eventually led to the last kid left, and she then had to be the first It.

One of the more injury prone games was called "Red Rover" and often ended on someone getting hurt enough to cry or quit the game. Red Rover was played by two sides lining up and facing until the challenge was issued: "Red Rover, Red Rover, send Louise, (or whoever was chosen) right over." With the name called out, the person was supposed to run at the other line, slam into a weak spot, and break through. This game didn't last very long before we wanted to play something less damaging to ourselves. There was another game called "Sling the Statue" where the one who was It had to grab a kid by the arm, spinning and turning as hard as possible and then letting go, but the one being slung had to freeze as if a statue. I have no idea at all what the purpose or goal of that game was, it wasn't one of my favorites. We had a chase and taunting game called "Devil in the Ditch" but that game relied on having a sidewalk to serve as the ditch. Whoever was It had to try and tag one of the others as they dashed across the sidewalk, or tried to jump over it without being caught. Most of the more aggressive games probably served a good cause, to let children who were held in check most of the day blow off some of their pent-up energy in ways that didn't get us in trouble with the grownups in our lives, especially since we were all raised in the "don't talk back" school of parenting.

Then there was the most creative of all our games, "Mother May I" where the It called out a child by name and instructed her, or him if we were allowing boys to play, to take a certain number of steps forward and in a prescribed manner, such as two giants steps or three duck walks. That was a great game for stirring creativity and often led to arguments about how well the steps were being performed or even if such steps could be judged. There was one game that could only be played while calling out a certain chant: "Ain't no boogers out tonight, Grandpa killed 'em all last night" at which point everyone was supposed to dash madly around in the yard trying to evade being caught, and then becoming It. I think that game, Boogers, has a history and a meaning that might reach back into a darker time and carry some message that is more than child's play. However accustomed to playing out at night, in our familiar territory, there was still a chill felt as a child to be outside, in the dark, running around in a neighbor's yard or your own and without any adults in charge. There was just enough of risk implied in that game of Boogers, or Boogeyman to keep us all playing it. Those were some of the warm weather outdoor games that kept us all flinging ourselves about being as free range as we wanted. There were other games, played indoors or when the big sisters were in charge and wanted to bring in some of their new discoveries, but these were our typical summer night entertainment.

One of the other ways to spend time outside in the summer night was to lie on a blanket in the front yard and look at the sky, watching for whatever magic might appear in the dark summer night. The adults often came outside to sit while the house cooled a little after the supper was cooked and eaten, fans were left on inside and it was a time for a little relaxing, maybe visiting a little with neighbors, but mostly just being outside in the cooling night. Sitting on the front porch and speaking with neighbors was the entertainment before television and air conditioners were in every home in the South. Pitchers of ice water were taken out to the porch, fans were aimed at the porch swing, and the family sat down – the adults of the family sat, not the children. We were ramping up our games and trying to cram another hour or two of boisterous playing before the mamas started calling kids by name, telling us it was time to come in – the street lights were on and time to come home.

One of the risks we faced in running around the yards and streets at night was the damage done to bare feet since most of us eschewed any shoes during the summer, until Sunday morning when we were all required to attend Sunday School at our various but consistently Protestant churches. Out of all the children in my neighborhood, only one family was not Protestant: the Tully family was Roman Catholic. They were a lovely family who lived at the top of my street and Rosemary, the daughter my age, attended the parochial school in West End. She was the only kid in the neighborhood who presented even the slightest variation in our otherwise bland homogeneity. The rest of us were mostly Baptist, or Methodists, and a couple were Presbyterian, but we all had to clean up and be presentable on Sunday morning. Where the mandatory Sunday morning "dress up" became a problem was when the damage done to bare feet had to be reckoned with by trying to jam band-aid covered toes into stiff patent leather shoes. No excuse worked, no amount of pain counted, those shoes were for Sunday School and it was Sunday. I was taken to Sunday School every Sunday with my grandmother, who attended her own women's class while I showed up for mine. I do not recall a single time of attending any church service with either of my parents, only my grandmother. Now, as an adult, I can see that was a time for them to have the only privacy possible in a small house of eight people.

As soon as my class ended, I would race up the stairs, slip in the door, and take the empty seat next to my grandmother while we all recited the benediction:

May the words of my mouth and the meditations of my heart be always acceptable

In Thy sight, oh Lord my strength and my redeemer. Psalm 19

After all those years, the words that I recited with the women of her Sunday School class remain fresh in my mind, rolling off my tongue without hesitation. She was a rock steady presence in my life, the one who took me to church, the one always at home while the other adults were away at work, and the one who gave me the nickel to spend on Mr. Dunn's rolling grocery store.

Mr. Dunn, the housewife's best friend, had a bus that had been converted to carry the essentials for daily needed foods such as bread, fresh produce, and Marita snack cakes. The Marita devil's food cake cost five cents and was usually my choice for spending the nickel. Sometimes I would buy a Butterfinger or Baby Ruth candy bar from Mr. Dunn's bus, but the chocolate cake with white filling was my favorite. My grandmother often sent me out to the "truck" to buy for her, so the cake was earned. She was also quick to swat me with the business end of her broom if I didn't meet her expectations of behavior. My love for her was unlimited and abiding, and I think I failed to let her know that she was that dear to me. Maybe she understood it without my being able to say the words, maybe she knew from my frequently asking to come back to her house to spend the night with her after we had moved into our own house, or maybe she felt what I wasn't wise enough to tell, that I loved her and trusted her.

My grandmother came to Birmingham with her husband, W. C. Philips (Philips is often spelled either as Philips, or Phillips) around 1922, after several years of cotton crop failures had cost him his country store in Perry County, Alabama. I looked at the federal census schedules for 1910, 1920, 1930 and 1940 for his name to see where he and his family were living. In 1910 the census showed him living, in Scotts, Perry County, Alabama with his wife, Ella who he had married in 1904 and four others in the household. In their household were their two young sons Frank and Phil, and W.C.'s brother Randolph, age 18. Randolph was listed as working as a salesman. Since his brother W.C. operated a general store, I have assumed that Randolph worked in the same store owned by his older brother. There was one more name listed as a member of the household, a woman named Ellen Jackson, age 69, Black, and widowed. On the census schedule her work is listed as "cook" and her employer as "private family." I once heard my grandmother tell a brief bit of information about her home and life before they moved to Birmingham. She said that one of her children was extremely ill to the point that she had given up that child would recover, until, as she described the other person, until my grandmother turned the child's care over to "the woman who worked for me." I wonder if that was Ellen Jackson. Did Ellen Jackson, Black live-in cook, tend to and nurse back to health one of my uncles or my aunt or even my mother? I will not ever know, but I choose to write her name to honor all the Ellen Jacksons who tended and cared for and perhaps saved the child of the White woman for whom she worked.

In 1910 W.C. owned his own home free of any debt or mortgage for it and ran his store in Perry County and farmed a little as well. By the next decade, 1920 some changes had taken place, and they were downward turning ones for him and his family; he was no longer operating the store, his employment was listed as farming, and he no longer owned a house but was renting one. There was no servant listed and his brother's name is no longer carried as a part of the household. It's easy for me to assume that the boll weevil infestations that destroyed cotton crops in the period around 1915 to 1920 had cost him his store. Crop losses effected the credit economy of the cotton South in a wide ripple across rural counties and since small merchants like W.C. lived by credit they lost out as well as the farmers. Those farmers who planted and harvested their crops did so on the credit from the local furnishing merchant, as he was, and he in turn depended on credit from his bank or larger merchants. If the farmers couldn't pay the store then the store owner couldn't pay his debts either. This crop failure led to the share cropping farmers leaving the rural South for the industrial North and the cities were where workers were in demand. The steady northern flow of African American share croppers to industrial urban areas is often called The Diaspora or The Great Migration by historians because so many Black farmers and most especially farm workers left the agricultural South and moved to Detroit, Chicago, Cleveland, Pittsburg and so many other cities, along with many White farmers and their families. The timing of the migration seems to have been the result of a combination of failing cotton crops starting in 1915 and the later need of industrial workers for World War II, so essentially the heaviest loss of agricultural workers from South to North was between 1915 and 1940 and eventually reached totals around five million. My grandfather made a similar move, going not so far as Detroit or Columbus, Ohio, or any of the northern cities: he moved his family to the still-growing city of Birmingham, Alabama. He took a job there with that mighty co-founder of the "Magic City" – the Louisville & Nashville Railroad.

Birmingham had two parents; pig iron and the rail lines that hauled it. Iron production soon gave way to the manufacture of steel, and the railroads eventually gave way to paved roads for automobiles, but Birmingham was a city created for a single purpose; to mine coal and red iron ore to feed the furnaces. Birmingham also offered a new chance for those men and women who were tired and displaced after the Civil War ended. I know the story of the city so well that I could write a thousand pages just about where I was born and grew up, and all that came before that 1943 event on Easter Sunday, but I am not here for that. I am here to tell my own personal story. Birmingham will always be in my memories, a part of my heart and there will always be some of that blood red iron ore dust in my bones and blood, but I do not live there now. Except for my brother no one in my close kinship clan remain in the city. Those who have "walked on down the road" (as a friend speaks of dying) and whose bodies lie in the red mother earth of Jefferson County are all that remain of my relatives there, and I do not visit their graves. Unlike my mother and my aunt Sissy, who spent many Sunday afternoons at Elmwood Cemetery tending the graves of their departed loved ones, I do not.

Tending the graves of those departed ones was a woman's job. Women went to the cemeteries and planted pansies, and pulled weeds from around the graves. The women in my family would sit by the resting places and talk to each other, about current matters or in memories of their still remembered ones, or being silent in that place rightly called in German a "Friedhof" - a peace yard. It is peaceful to sit in silence in an open expanse of land where there is no vehicle traffic or loud activities taking place, to remember the life of someone who lives on in memory and just be. I said that tending the graves is a woman's job because that is my own experience as a child and later as an adult woman living in Germany where I became aware of how often on Saturday in the late afternoon, I saw women of an older generation walking down the sidewalks, carrying a small bunch of cut flowers. Only on Saturdays did I see them, and soon I came to understand that they were headed for the cemeteries, where so many of their dead were buried. They were the generation left when the war took their men and left them behind to visit the graves. It was the work of the women to feed the living, and remember the dead. We were the keepers of the family both in life and then in memory. We are still the keepers of the stories.

In the Spring Sissy, Mother, Jane and I would go to the cemetery where my grandfather's body was buried, and while my mother and aunt did their bit of gardening around the site, Jane and I ran around the one especially big and tall pecan tree that stood near our family plot. Elmwood had sections of land not dedicated to grave sites, where one could see rather odd things like a huge concrete mushroom tall enough to sit under it and a little footbridge over only grass. I think that bridge was a symbolic reminder of the kind of place we were visiting, the one for those who had "crossed over a bridge" or maybe it was just someone's idea of what was appropriate for a graveyard. I do know that spending so much time in that peaceful and decorated place gave me a deep sense of the cemetery as a place quiet and restful, a gentle park.

To consider a graveyard as a park was a deliberate move in the late nineteenth century in the United States intended to create a vision of the burying ground as a park rather than the grim boneyard as it was called in the past. It worked for me as a place of respite. I have often visited cemeteries in places where I was new or just visiting because of my pleasant association with them as a place where the veil between the worlds is thin and lovely. And it serves to remind me of what so many wise ones tell us: we do not show up from nowhere, from no one. We all come from long lines of ancestors and we will one re-enter that stream of energy and become a memory. Phap Dung, a Buddhist monk said of the approach of death for his mentor Thich Nhat Hanh, that we all have roots, and ancestors and are part of a stream. Most of the women of my mother's generation tended the graves of their families and I am glad to have had that connection with the past, that sense of the continuity of family that I learned as a child in the cemetery with the women.

I don't know if my grandmother ever returned to the old burying grounds in Perry County to visit or tend the graves of her mother Emma or her father Solomon, and I don't know if she was able to visit the graves of her sister Mamie who died so young at the age of only twenty years in 1895. My grandmother, called "Mammaw" by all of her six grandchildren, Betty Ann, Janice, Hal, Jane, Eddie and

I, was born in 1883 and was the fifth in a family of eleven children. Mamie was the first born and very beautiful. I have an old miniature of her painted on a porcelain oval, with her sweet smile and calm eyes seeming to gaze out at eternity, and I wonder if it was done as a loving way to remember her after her death. I can't know now, I never thought to ask anyone who did know when I had time enough to have heard the stories of her life, and I was too young to believe that death was real and would come to all of us on one day or another. Had I asked Mammaw, she would have known, she would have been able to tell me about her beautiful older sister who had died.

It is good when children do not have to become acquainted with death at an early age, before they have lived long enough to have memories of those who make up a part of their story. I can still remember the first death to touch my life in 1953 and it was a very long time ago, but I remember Peter Jebeles. He was a classmate of mine in the elementary school I attended in West End. Pete and I went to Stonewall Jackson Elementary School with grades from first through eighth and made up of a very homogenous White and almost exclusively Protestant student body where a kid like Pete was the exception since his parents had been born in Greece and immigrated to the United States and were members of a Greek Orthodox congregation. The irony of the two of us children of immigrants attending a school named for a one who favored the practice of White supremacy which had been embraced by Southern states in the anti bellum era was lost on us. At age 10 we knew nothing about such political matters, knew only that our school was named for one of the generals of the Confederate military forces in the Civil War. In our town of Birmingham, memories of the Civil War were still being honored sixty years after its' end when Jackson Elementary School was constructed in 1925 and veterans of that war still marched in parades in downtown Birmingham.

We also knew nothing of the other Jackson, President Andrew Jackson, who had destroyed the powerful Alabama Muscogee tribes at what came to be known as the Battle of Horseshoe Bend in 1814. We had never heard of the battle, or the Trail of Tears, or about the brilliant William Weatherford, called Red Eagle or Lamochattee in his Muscogee language and had not the slightest knowledge of who had occupied the land our school and homes sat on, and no one in our education system taught us that history. In spite of that lacuna in our knowledge of our state history we were still in class together, Peter the descendant of Greek emigrants and Carol the descendant of German and Irish ones, together in a school named in honor of a man who will forever be remembered for his role in fighting to keep slavery alive in Alabama, Thomas J. "Stonewall" Jackson. It would two more years after Pete's death before I would encounter the name William Weatherford in my required course of Alabama History in the sixth grade and even then, reading how he was described in the state-sanctioned textbook, I intuitively rejected what I was reading as not true. Weatherford was the son of a Creek woman of high status and a father of European ancestry. Weatherford followed the custom of his mother's culture at age thirteen by undergoing a rite of passage to be accepted as a full male adult in his mother's clan. However, what I read in that biased textbook was that at thirteen, he "became a traitor to his people" which meant he did not choose to follow White culture and society, rather his choice was to follow his mother's linage. When he became an adult, he was the warrior who led the Red Sticks in battle as they carried blood red war clubs.

> *Red Sticks, the name deriving from the red-painted war clubs of some Native American Creeks – refers to an early 19th century traditionalist faction of these people in the American Southeast.* Wikipedia.

Neither Pete nor I knew about him when we were in Jackson School together. We just knew each other.

The Jebeles family was known to my family for a couple of reasons with one being we lived in the same community of West End at a time when it was more like a small town than a neighborhood. As I stated a bit earlier, there have been many books and articles, both popular and scholarly ones, published which offer analyses of the workforce of Birmingham from its founding in 1871 to the World War II era, with most of the studies offering break downs of the work force to include the racial and ethnic make-up of the different neighborhoods. However, the kids in the 4th grade at Jackson school such as Pete and I were not interested in how the community came to be, we were just kids together in school. I suspect that between my parents and grandmother, my family must have known half of the families of West End, or so it seemed to me because they sure knew the family of every kid I knew.

The other reason his family was known to my dad came from Daddy's time working as a deliveryman for a bread company when he had a route that included many of the little stores owned and operated by some of the Greek families of Birmingham. There were other families and my sister and I were in high school with the children of the Jebeles and Likis families, but Pete Jebeles remains in memory because he died at age ten and I was stunned. The kids in class together were aware that Pete was different from the rest of us in only one way: his physical appearance was a reflection of the heart abnormality which was gave him a delicate frame with pale skin and prominent blue veins. He was prevented from any of the rambunctious recess games we liked to play. In spite of his obvious delicate appearance, I never thought he was in danger of dying young and I remember that night after I had learned of his death. I wept at the supper table, and there was no comfort for me in being in the midst of my own family. I couldn't believe that my sweet, fragile friend would not be in class ever again.

The table where we sat for evening meals was a large one with two sections that could be added to expand it, however without the extra sections it was still large enough for the five adults and (eventually) three children. Everyone had their own place and we sat in the same places at that table. My grandmother sat at the head, flanked on each side by a daughter and son-in-law, and my sister and I sat side-by-side at the foot, facing her. I do not remember where Eddie sat, maybe near his grandmother, but I cannot recall. The house was small for such a large family. There was an "L" shaped porch across the front that ran a short distance down one side, to a doorway into the dining room. A swing hung from the ceiling on the side porch and once my dad and I sat in the swing watching a thunder storm approaching, with all the lightning and thunder that would have terrified me as young as I was had he not taught me how to appreciate the power and beauty of the storm and told me how to count between the lightning bolt flash and the thunder. If I had to describe a scene of total confidence and sense of safety as a child, it would be that experience. Once the space was enclosed for a bedroom there was place for the swing anymore and the only door into the room opened from the dining room. But to go back to the layout of the house, the front door opened off the front porch and into the living room, where there was a small fireplace which, by the time I was aware held a small gas burner and was flanked on each side by windows that opened onto the side portion of the wrap-around L-shaped porch. Leaving the living room toward the right was the dining room, then a small breakfast room with a built-in cabinet at one end and a window at the other, then into the kitchen with a pantry and finally out the door onto a narrow room where the double-tubs and wringer washing machine sat. There was a door out to the backyard from that small room. That small room was also the area where the men sat in the fall of the year after coming home from squirrel hunting. They sat there to skin the squirrels so that the women could cook them for our dinner. I often sat with them, watching how they cleaned the game, listening to them talk about their hunting.

On the left side of the house, leaving the living room was the first bedroom, my parents' room, and also where my brother's crib was, and then a small hallway, a bathroom, then the second bedroom, and just beyond that second bedroom where my sister and I shared one bed and our grandmother had a separate bed. There was a small night stand between the two beds with a radio on the little shelf below the top of the stand. This is where Jane and I spent a lot of time listening to radio programs at night. Each of us would lie on the floor, in the dark with the radio on, each under a separate bed and listen to a variety of radio programs: The Green Hornet, Boston Blackie, Superman, The Lone Ranger, The Inner Sanctum, and The Shadow were our favorites, although the squeaking door sound that signaled the start of the Inner Sanctum never failed to frighten me before the show ever started. In the next room which lay just beyond my grandmother's was what served as a bedroom for Sissy and Papa and probably had originally been a screened-in porch, but as long as far back as I can remember it was the third bedroom. Papa had a radio in that room also and would lie on the bed listening to baseball games. There were several radios in our house, even a large short-wave radio that probably came from Mr. Greene, one of the men who owned the real estate company where Sissy was a secretary. I tried using it a few times, and it was exciting to hear the static and distant voices, wondering where in the world the speaker was. Someone owned a record player that sat in the living room. I heard "Mississippi Mud" many times played on that record player, and a few other songs as well.

When I was about 6 or 7 a fourth bedroom was created when the men in our family and Mr. Davis, the next-door neighbor who was a builder, enclosed the side porch for Jane and I to share (the same side porch where the swing once was). The Davis family was Mr. and Mrs. Davis and their three sons, Ray, Jimmy, and Tom. Ray was a bit older than my sister, Jimmy was my age and the first crush of my childhood, and Tom was my brother Eddie's best friend for many years. They moved from that neighborhood before we did, but Eddie and Tom long remained friends. My mother told me that because Mrs. Davis had wished for a daughter but not had one, she liked to help my mother make my dresses. My mother was quite adept at sewing and made most of my clothes when I was young. Mom would make the dress, and Mrs. Davis finished it with smocking on the bodice. One of our photos of my mother, sister, and I, taken as a Father's Day gift for my dad, shows me in one of those smocked dresses. They were good neighbors and I have sweet memories of the special attention she paid me.

The bedroom that Mr. Davis had a hand in constructing was small, just wide enough for a double bed to fit in the end of the room, but was adequate for Jane and I to sleep in and thus give my grandmother a bedroom to herself. When the house was built there was a fire place in the living room, flanked by two windows, one on each side of the upper part with built-in book cases beneath each window in the living room. When that part of the porch was enclosed, the windows were left but always closed. However, my sister and I could, and did, stand on our bed just beneath the window and listen to what the grown-ups were talking about on the other side of the window, in the living room. We thought we were getting away with something and were so amused at our little trick. Once Jane and I moved into that bedroom, our grandmother had her own bedroom, located right between the two married daughters' and their husbands. I still think about how well they seemed to manage in that house, and how little privacy was available for five adults and three children and one bathroom.

For a few years there was no house on the other side of Mammaw's, just a vacate lot that became our neighborhood baseball field. We did what most children of our time and location in suburban America did, we played baseball and football without any adult involvement or supervision, so we made up and enforced our own rules. One rule was that any ball hit over the sidewalk and into the street was an automatic homerun. Another rule was that I was the designated runner for my sister's best friend Vivian Fondrin. Vivian had a bad knee and could not run so I was her runner. She was also the youngest child in her family of three children and their house was the last one on 16th Place, with first two then three houses between ours and theirs. The other two houses were the Pattersons and the Averrits. The Pattersons were Red, Margurite, and their only child Priscilla and the Averrits were the parents (whose names I have forgotten) and their three children Lamar, Carol Ann, and a younger brother. Many of my misadventures involved Jimmy Davis, Lamar Averrit, and I while we were quite young. Later after Jimmy Davis had moved I had less to do with Lamar and spent my time with the girls in the neighborhood. However, there is one memorable event that took place with we three, Jimmy, Lamar, and I which was pretty funny to me now, but not to the adults when they found out about it. We were standing in the alley behind Lamar's house when I decided I wanted to know what made girls and boys different so I proposed we reveal our covered parts to each other, and my exact words were "I'll show you mine if you show me yours." They complied, we all took a good look and that was the end of it – until Lamar told his parents! I got some kind of reprimand from my mother, but not much else other than recognizing that Lamar was a tattletale and Jimmy was not.

There were other kids in the neighborhood, some were there the entire ten years I lived there, such as Louise and Marion Sellers across the street and the Tully children all the way up at the end of the block in the opposite direction from the Pattersons and Averrits. Louise was my best friend until we moved and then she switched her loyalty to one of my new neighbors in our new place three blocks away. The Tullys were Roman Catholic and Rosemary, my friend who was my age, attended the Catholic school Sacred Heart in West End while the rest of the Protestant Children in the neighborhood went to Jackson – Stonewall Jackson – the public school. Most of us who lived at our end of the street walked to school together every day until the older ones moved on to high school. The house we lived in, my grandmother's, sits at the point where two streets met, where one street angled into 16th Place. The other street was Cleburn Avenue, where the Sellars lived and a couple of houses down from them was the house where my parents were married in 1936. I don't know why they were married in that house, unless someone in her family was renting it. And a bit farther down Cleburn were some other families with children about my age, and my sister's age. There was another family named Patterson on Cleburn, whose older child was my sister's age, she was in the same sorority in high school as Jane and the son was Ralph, who was my age and who graduated from Jackson Elementary at the same time as I in January, 1957. Chris Hopkins lived next door to Ralph but I have no memory of his family. Across the street from those two houses lived the Satterfields, who had 2 or 3 children but we were not friends.

As I mentioned above the two streets were Cleburn and 16th Place SW and the Tullys lived up the slightly inclined 16th Place. Within the triangular patch created by the intersection of the two streets and the short extension of 16th Place down to the alley, were between 20 and 25 houses which comprised my world until we moved the 3 blocks away to 1418 16th Way SW. And the alley which extended all the length of 16th Place SW was a place where we children spent a lot of time, searching for discarded but returnable glass soda bottles and what other treasures we might find. Children are natural scavengers and treasure hunters, and take delight in discovery. We once found a litter of dead newborn kittens in the alley behind the Waldrop house, so we buried them. Being left up to our own entertainment gave us the time to wander, to discover, and to create our own small world where we had control without any adult presence. I am still in favor of kids getting this so-called free-range childhood. When I became a parent, it was the natural way for my own children to be allowed that kind of freedom.

The Waldrop house held something of a mystery for me, a family not quite like my own, but not so different that they were off-limits for me. The family was somewhat like my own, a three-generation family living in one moderate house together, but with a couple of differences that seemed significant to me at the time: the older man, the one who was a grandfather would not eat meals with his grandchildren. The children had to wait until he had eaten before they could come to the dinner table and if that was not different enough, his daughter, who was the mother of those children, played softball! I had never known an adult woman who lived a life which differed in the very slightest detail from that of my own mother and aunt and all their women relatives and friends. By the time I was ten years old, I had led such a culturally homogeneous life that I literally was amazed that an adult woman would spend time playing softball with other women. I wonder now if she lived other small differences that were not apparent to me. Young children tend to accept what they are told and what they see at "face value" and seldom question the validity of the received culture. I must have had some doubts about what I saw because I remember that she played softball – not a strange or bizarre activity – but one that was a little bit at odds with the rest of the women I knew. And there was one other moment where I was told something by my parents that I knew as they were saying it to me that what they were saying was not true. I did not know what the truth was, only that in a flash of intuitive knowledge, they were covering up something.

Their little lie was about my friend Rosemary Tully's mother, who I noticed had a large belly, but no fat anywhere else. I asked my parents about that because it looked odd to me, who was all of 7 or 8 years old, and I have a very clear memory of that moment: the two of them standing near the open front door and glancing at each other when I asked, probably each one waiting to see what the other one was going to say, how to approach the secrets of sex and pregnancy with which both must have been very uncomfortable having to answer a question that might lead to more questions, me being the child in the family infamous for asking "too many questions." I think it was my mother who finally responded with a weak explanation that "oh, people can just gain weight like that, in different places." I stood there, wondering why they were lying to me, because while I did not know what the truth was, I knew I was not hearing it. Sex was never discussed, no information given to me about any of the normal events of my life as I matured, no simple answers that would leave open a door that later in my life I would actually need to approach them when I really needed advice. My parents were probably typical of the middle-class mores and culture of silence around sexual activity and birth control which left girls my age in the dark about much we should have been told long before the ignorance led to so many of us facing an unplanned and unwanted teen-age pregnancy.

The Tullys also had one other tradition that differed from ours and that was how they celebrated Christmas. It was their custom to attend a midnight Mass on Christmas Eve, and when they returned Santa had made his visit. Our family did not attend church on Christmas Eve or day, and Santa left our gifts sometime during the early morning. The children in the family, Jane, Eddie, and I, all hung stockings from the mantel over the small fireplace. My father had the heart of a child when it came to Christmas and loved to be a part of the celebrations. He gave each of us one of his long socks that he wore under his snake proof boots which he wore when he went hunting. His boots laced up the front almost to his knees, so he had pretty long socks to wear, and pretty long socks to hold more presents from Santa. Christmas was usually a happy day full of visits from relatives and kids playing outside with their new skates, or bikes, BB guns. The biggest Christmas disappointment of my childhood was that I never got the cowgirl boots that I had wanted for several years. There is another memory from Christmas that is not good, that sort of haunts me; my mother gave away one of my gifts without asking me.

One of my gifts that particular Christmas morning was a sterling silver oval shaped hair clasp that I found rather beautiful. It was still in the gift box, under the tree where I left it after opening. When the family who lived across the street, Dardens I think, came over to give me a gift and my mother realized she had not prepared for that, grabbed my new yet-unworn silver hair clasp and gave it to the young daughter I was silently angry with her. Possibly I would have agreed to do that if she had asked, but she was not the kind of parent who gave my 8-year-old autonomy any respect. She often acted in ways that now, as an adult, I can easily see were based on her worry about approval. My grandmother, her mother, must have been a strict parent who had not given her own daughter much say in many matters and since my mother was living in the house owned by her mother, there must have been a lot of unacknowledged and unexpressed tension between them. I do know that my mother held a deep core value that to argue within the family, to create disturbance within the household was to be avoided at all costs. So, in order to protect her own standing with the neighbors, she diminished me. I never told her how I felt about that loss of a gift, but also never forgot that she did it. I wonder if any of my own children could say that about me?

One other memory about Christmas and then I will mentally wave good-bye to that topic. My mother had 3 siblings, Alvice (with whom we lived), Frank Howell (who was the eldest and called "Brother" by the two sisters), and Phil. One year we were to eat dinner at Phil's house, but my dad had gone to Montgomery to see the annual Blue-Gray football game, so he was a bit late getting back and we were all sitting down to eat, already at the table when he came in. I was seated next to his place, and saw that there some odd things at his place, odd things that Papa (Sissy's husband and my dad's brother-in-law) had put there as a joke. He had put plastic ice cubes with what looked like bees and flies into Daddy's water glass, rubber olives on his plate, and a fork that collapsed when picked up. Papa was watching Daddy as he began to eat, picking up the fork, and then Papa burst into laughter, unable to keep the secret of who did it. They had such a good time together, Daddy and Papa, they enjoyed each other's sense of humor and made all of us laugh.

No matter how well it worked, it came to an end in 1953 when I was ten, my sister fifteen, my bother five. We moved three blocks away from 1241 16th Place into our own, separate home at 1418 16th Way, SW which was (and as of this day in 2019 still is) across the street from Jackson Elementary. I lived there for the next eight years until I left for San Diego at age eighteen to marry. My neighborhood was where I spent most of my time outside of being in school and where both my brother and sister lived until each of them married. In my memory, each of the two houses seem to appear in rather different light, evoking different feelings when I think about each one, probably because of the age I was when living in each place and because of the family members with whom I lived.

The house at 1241 16th Place, my grandmother's house, was my first home and all of my earliest memories derive from that home, but after we moved into our own house, I met the neighbors and their children who made up my small, protected, and well-loved world. There were some houses which predated ours and some that were built after we moved into our own, new house that our old neighbor V.R. Davis built for us. The older houses were occupied by the Penningtons, the small rental house next to them, then the Grahams, then the Woodrows, our two lots, then two more open lots, the Melhorns, and two older houses which made up that side of the street. The last house on that side was occupied by a family we barely saw or ever knew named Moody. The families that lived across the street when we moved into our house were the Carlisles and one more at the top of the hill that I have forgotten the name of. After we moved in, there was a house built were next door, built by L.C. Wyatt who worked as a brick mason. His wife's father had been a barber in West End known to my parents, and when L.C. started work on his house my dad already knew the family. The house holds a story for me, one that reflects what neighborhoods were like.

L.C. had reached a point in the construction (which he was doing largely on his own) when he suddenly was lost about what to do next. Somehow my dad learned that, as I remember Daddy walked next door to see how the construction was going, only to find L.C. in tears of total frustration. Daddy, Cotton Roy, Frank Graham, and Ed Melhorn joined in to help him work on the construction and get past his frustration. After the house was completed and the Wyatt's moved in, they lived there a while and then sold it to another family whose son Caspar became a part of the neighborhood gang of kids who hung out together. There are two more particular memories attached to that house: one is the day Cotton fell out of a tree that he was trimming and the second is the day the house caught fire. Cotton's fall from the tree was especially seared into my memory because I was standing near the tree and saw him fall from it, hit the paved driveway below and bounce.

It had been the same when Cotton was building his house across the street from where L.C.'s lot lay. The older men in the neighborhood helped him with the construction at some time. Cotton was a football coach at West End High, where my sister, my brother, and I all attended as we came of age for that schooling. He was a big part of my life from the time I was 11 or so until his death in 1968.

The bands of friendship and sharing among neighbors lasted a long time, long enough that after my father's death in 1966, and my mother's decision to build a new house and move from West End, she turned to L.C. to construct the house in a developing residential area "over the mountain" in Bluff Park. L.C. did build the house and refused to make a profit from it, telling her that he had a favor to repay, that he was able to start out as a builder because of the assistance that had been given him by my father. My mother lived in the Bluff Park house from 1970 until her death in June, 2009. Her sister had sold her house, the one that had been my first home, and they went in together to pay for and live in the new home in Bluff Park. For a while her son Hal lived there with them but he later moved to a small apartment in the Five Points South area of Birmingham. By the time of her death in 2009, my mother had lived alone in the house after Sissy's passing in 1998 and Hal's in 2002. My mother did not want anyone to live with her and adamantly refused to even consider moving to an independent living apartment. Until her death she regarded such an apartment as some kind of place where old people were warehoused, waiting to die. I think she must have had memories of that kind of place from her rural childhood. She most certainly would not have ever been "warehoused" by her children because until she was 90, she was healthy and very lively. At

90 she had a pace maker for a condition that robbed her of that previous vitality, dying at age 93. The last 3 years of Mom's life I saw a decline in her physical health and a deep malaise set in that seldom lifted.

As I write these memories into an existence independent of my private memories, I am drawn back to the links that my family had with the families around Pete Jebeles who had died too young at age 10. These connections reveal a community life that bound so many families in a common life where our lives were lived in a stable and secure environment of schools, places of worship, small family businesses, and a similar economic status. His parents, siblings and cousins who went on to West End High School with me, my siblings, and all my cousins. West End High was established in 1930 so that the high school aged children of our community would not have to continue traveling to Phillips High in down town Birmingham. My aunt Sissy had attended Phillips but when time came for my mother, who was 3 years her junior, to start high school, West End High's construction was complete and my mother must have been in the first class to enter the 9th grade at that school. Sissy graduated from Phillips in 1931 and one of her classmates was a pretty young woman named Alma who soon married Sissy's brother Phil but my mother did not graduate. Instead, she dropped out in her senior year. She once told me that her reason for leaving before graduating was because of her father's health. He had a stroke and could no longer work and she felt it necessary to leave school for a paying job to help support her parents.

My mother talked about her mother's family, the sisters Emma Edwards, Lucy Pack, Alvice Lavendar, and Annie Hardenburg who came to visit their sister Ella Howell in the big city. We usually celebrated holidays with my mother's two brothers Frank Howell and Phil Howell and her sister who we called Sissy and their spouses, but she had little to say about her own early life or to tell me about growing up in Birmingham, with a couple of exceptions. One story was so funny that we still talk about it. It is the one about something that happened before her father decided to leave Scotts in Perry County for Birmingham when she was six years old. This must have happened the last summer they lived there because she said she was about 6 and her cousins of the story were 4 and 7. In my mother's version of this event the blame lay primarily on four-year-old Golda and her red shoes, with Golda's brother Raymond as a partner in the event.

Like most children in the South at the time Mom went barefoot as long as the weather was mild enough, about 9 months out of the year but her little cousin was sporting these fine red shoes and bragged about them to her barefoot cousin once too often so my mother took action: she put her, red shoes and all, in the pig pen with the pigs. Of course, Golda screamed, the men came running, and she "told on" her cousin. My mother shrewdly assessed the situation and hit on another plan to be rid of her annoying tattle-tale cousin: she tried to set fire to the baby bed that was being used for the younger cousin. My mother told me that she could remember thinking that if the child had nowhere to sleep, they would have to leave and go away. Having done that and sensing that punishment had to come soon, my mother crawled under the house and refused to come out. My daughters have told that and told that story about their grandmother, and told it with some kind of pride that she was not a kid who was going to be intimidated easily.

My daughters love that story about their grandmother, who they had grown up knowing as an adult and through her stories they came to know in such a way that some of her story was embedded in their way of remembering her once she passed into memory and out of their lives. Why do we keep our stories? Do we need more than the facts, the data on paper that shows where someone was born, and in which year she was married and which was her first house? And what role does the story play in recounting history or remembering from one's own personal memories? How do we separate memory from history and should they be pulled apart? I have been mulling over this question about how my memory functions and why I hold on to some of my memories even after I have learned that there are facts that just do not line up with the way I remember an event or person or place. And yet, that memory or those memories are so important to me, contain so much energy and power for me that I cannot let go of them. Why? And now I know the answer for my question; those memories give life to my story; they are blood and flesh on the bones of the facts. Our memories are the life blood that runs through our family generation to generation, from my mother, and my father and those who came before.

Memory needs some help, a way to keep the details in order and to keep telling the story in the same order every time. There are many ways to do that and one way, especially for those who tell the stories out of memory rather than from a written form, is to use a mnemonic device. The Roman Catholic Church has a great mnemonic device that is called the "rosary" where a chain has beads that are strung in such a manner as to remind the one holding the rosary in hand what comes next, which prayer follows on after the first and then the next and all the way to the finish. The griots of West Africa have a knotted cord where each knot is like a bead on the rosary and each story is preserved in an oral tradition aided by the mnemonic device. Another way was what Plains tribes did when they told stories or set down events on their buckskin shirts or the bison hide tipi. Other cultures used rocks to peck out symbols, events, or what might have been directions left from one nomadic clan on the move to another one to follow. The meaning of many of the symbols left on rock surfaces, petroglyphs, are unknown to us now, but certainly had meaning for those who created them. Some might have just been the way of saying "We were here" to relatives and were perhaps explanations of family relations, I am not certain about the family story idea, but I have seen the figures etched and picked onto cliff faces and figures painted on tipis and shirts that are clearly meant to convey an account of past events. Other cultures kept their stories though a variety of media such as in songs or sagas that told of the heroes of their linage and another way was that of the troubadour who walked about with a lute or some musical instrument and sang songs that told specific stories, carrying tales and news around Europe.

I also have another form of remembering and it is my National Park Passport that is worn and running out of clean pages or space for the stamps that show where I have visited sites in the National Park system. Until I met a Park Ranger who was Nez Perce and the keeper of the museum of his tribe, I did not see the real function of my tattered passport. He gave me the way of seeing it as my rosary, my way of recalling my travels and my way of touching the past as often as I wanted. Now, although I did not write down all of my adventures or travels or personal discovery as they were occurring, I can look at the Passport and be reminded of each story contained in my memory that needed a bit of jogging to recall. I know enough about how we want to keep our memories and history and make it into our story to see the importance of mnemonic devices.

There is one more memory that shines a light into the past for me, one more device that visually told in one strong look with no written or painted or knotted help all the story of those in whose memory it was created. It happened like this: I was traveling in the West and the Plains states with my traveling companion and I noticed on the map that we were going to be close to a place that I knew about, from history but not memory, and a place I shied away from seeing, the Little Bighorn. The Battle, the Massacre, the fierce place of warriors meeting warriors that represented only death and loss to me, was close by and we had all the time needed to stop and step out onto that sacred ground should we choose to do that. I really didn't want to see it, yet felt such a strong pull, an urge to make the stop and somehow pay homage to…what? To whom? I didn't know, I only knew that my inarticulate intuition was pressing me to make the stop. Because I learned to listen to that intuition a long time ago, we stopped.

Right here is the best place to add a sidebar about my relationship with battlefields and military hero worship. I have a conflicted and lively feeling about how we Americans endow all things military with a special glow of almost mythic power, as if every man (and I mean male adult human here, women were seldom allowed into that mighty memorial of Valhalla in our American minds) who wore the uniform was automatically granted special status, as if every man on the western frontier was a brave and courageous fighter for, oh, stop, I can't do that. I have read too much history, too much factual data, and heard too many stories about the lethal encounters between the technology of the late nineteenth century American cavalry and mounted infantry against the essentially stone age technology of the Plains tribes, masters of light cavalry and warriors extraordinaire on horseback that they were, but still the outcome of their clash was inevitably destruction of the cultures of the tribes. Now on top of that acquired knowledge add on the experiential knowledge of being the woman of a warrior who in 1972 went to war in his army uniform and returned. I knew too much about Custer to admire him, and I knew what happened on that battleground in June of 1876 while most of the rest of the nation was observing the centennial of our political birth as a nation; the end of the Plains cultures was at hand.

Yet something urged me to face this site. As Mac walked toward the small hilltop memorial, I faltered, walking slowly toward the little building serving as a visitors' center. No one was inside the small room, but my attention fell on the glass case in the room, which held what looked a model of the battle site. Inside the case was a mock-up of the larger hill outside, and was made to resemble a small hillside with two streams flowing around the mound and joining at the base and forming one larger stream. Over the joined streams, where they met and flowed into one, was a structure which looked like the kind of signs you can see in the west, the name of the place that the road will lead you if you pass through the gate. The small label on this model read "Spirit Gate Where the warriors spirits met and became one." The artist-builder, a Lakota, had offered the model to show how to honor all of the warriors from both sides of the battle and a way remember them without words. I stood in silence for a while, thinking about this vision of the one who made the model and in agreement that as we pass through the spirit gate of death, we do become part of the entire flow of energy that does not distinguish between those passing through. I have not passed through that gate yet and do not know how it will be, but since so many of those who were so much a part of my past have done so, I am curious about it.

Returning to my mother's story about the annoying cousin and putting her in the pig pen, I was told the story in a certain way and probably over time perhaps I filled in some of gaps with what I thought happened or what maybe my mom said, and told it that way so many times but recently I have relied on documentary evidence available on the internet, so I could look up the names and ages of the cousins before I wrote about them. This is where I have to pause and consider what chimera I am chasing. My mother had a story that revealed something about her life and her memories of her childhood. For it to be valuable to her and then to me, how would I treat it? Should it be verified with a footnote attached or should I love it and burnish it in the re-telling? What I decide to do with her stories depends on how I value them, whether they help me see who she once was as a child or would I choose to write about her in a flat historic and rather lifeless manner? If I am after the real breathing person to know their blood red life then I shall choose to do what poet Emily Dickinson advised, to tell the truth but tell it slant. I have told her story but now have a few facts to help flesh out the real people of the story.

My mother was always clear about the ages of the cousins and her own age when her story took place, maybe her way of seeing what they had done in the context of being so young that they weren't very wise. Putting a child in a pig's pen is not something an older child would do, so I think she wanted us to know that she was really too young to have known it was a terrible idea and that particular cousin was never one she liked, even as an adult. The two cousins were Golda and Raymond, the children of her father's sister Pearl. As best I can reconstruct the family, Pearl and her four children, which included Raymond and Golda, were living with Pearl's parents Thomas Benton Howell (my maternal great-grandfather) and Mary Ella Archer Howell (my maternal great-grandmother) when the census taker came to her parents' home in Scotts, Perry County, Alabama in February of 1920. They were on the census schedule as present there, so I think that was true. And the census also shows that the next home to be enumerated was that of her brother William Carl Howell and his wife, Ella Phillips Howell, who were my maternal grandparents. There were three members of the Howell family living close to each that winter month, and I believe it was that same year that W.C. and Ella themselves left Scotts, in Perry County and moved their family to Birmingham. Pearl's husband was listed in the city directories of Birmingham as holding different jobs, but always in Birmingham until the time of his death in 1930. I do not know why Pearl was living with her parents or how long she remained there, but long enough for my six-year-old mother to want them to leave. Parents tell their children little pieces, small snippets of their lives get handed on to their children who may remember the stories, or maybe not. Parents seldom tell their children the unpleasant details either. I do know that not long after the pig pen episode my mother, her sister and brothers, and her parents left the country life and moved to the city where they all remained the rest of their lives.

As children - if we do remember what we were told - we sort of mentally tuck the little pieces somewhere without any content or any way of knowing how to fit them in the larger picture of family life and how we all came to be in one place together, so this records search is giving me a better understanding of what was going on when my mom created this particular memory. There is one other story, really a memory of mine that revealed something more about my mother's life growing up in Birmingham that I think reflected her personality; what she told me about her mother taking in boarders and how she resented that. My mother did not like to reveal her true feelings if she thought that by doing so it would result in any kind of conflict, which perhaps that was typical of the era before our current "tell-all" time of too much being revealed. What would social media be if no one was willing to tell everyone intimate details of their life? My mother was not one to do that, so when she once blurted out to me that as a child her mother never had time for her after they moved to the city of Birmingham, I was too surprised to do more than just ask what she meant. She very curtly responded "boarders, she took in boarders and had to cook for them and was too busy." And with that, she slammed shut the door to telling me more about her learning to live in a new environment in a new place and signaled that she felt neglected by her own mother. End of discussion.

That desire to keep peace in the family seems to have been attached to some specific experiences of hers as well as being part of the general ethos of her era to keep what was personal quiet and unspoken. She would intervene in any family conversation that she perceived as becoming too heated, too combative and tell us to stop arguing, stop "fighting" as she called it. Always the one who to point out the nakedness of the emperor, I finally asked her why she was so sensitive to a little squabble and her reply again reflects one more way that living in Birmingham affected her when she told me why. Her father and brothers worked in an industrial city where the economy was based on heavy manual labor, so naturally labor unions were a part of their lives, especially since her dad and one brother worked for L & N, Louisville & Nashville, railroad company. I don't know why they argued about unions but their arguing must have been heated and often because she spoke about those arguments with a lot of passion herself. And my dad was adamantly anti-union. She wanted peace within her family, even at the expense of being open and saying what often needed to be said, should have been said, and was not. Many times. I heard her emphatically state there could be no fighting within the family.

I said that Daddy was anti-union. I adored my father and wanted to be as much like him is most ways, emulating his old-fashioned value of keeping one's word, or as he often said "a man's word is his bond" and of not borrowing money. Again, to quote him "it's easier to get than to pay back." His advice to me about how to manage my very skimpy resources was the classic conservative advice of "live within your means." In most areas I wanted to be as he was, but in two we diverged and we could never agree; labor unions and race. I could understand his position on unions after he told me why he opposed them, but I thought his point of view was uncharacteristically myopic, but I could understand how he came to his point of view. His racism was never understandable and a painful aspect of a man I dearly loved. It was one topic we just could never have calm or objective discussions about, probably as much from my having no tolerance for it even with the person I loved most in life. While I cannot explain or justify his racism, I can say a little about his distrust of unions.

Keep in mind that my father worked in the iron ore and coal mining end of the steel industry in Birmingham, Alabama as most of the men of his family for generations. He worked in the commissary stores on Red Mountain, serving the mining camp communities, and his own father had been a "tally man" in one of the iron ore mines on that same mountain. His grandfather George W. had worked on the mountain, as did so many of his male cousins of the Lemley family and men of his mother's Curl family. Even his maternal grandfather, Burrel Curl was a blacksmith for one of the furnaces, so Daddy had seen the life of the hard labor of mining and making iron and steel, yet he failed to see a clear line of responsibility for the workers' health and well-being which led back to the failure of owners and managers to provide better care for the work force. The workers, especially those living in the mining camp communities did benefit from the paternalism of the social welfare typical of the era, but that was always a decision made for the work force, not by them. What Daddy saw, according to him, was that when the union called the men out on a strike, the workers would always lose. He told me about how the workers became so indebted to the company store during a strike that they could never be free of that debt. Rather than laying that at the door of the owners for failing to respect the unions primary concern of what is called a grievance, he could see only that the men and their families suffered if they struck.

There was one year when they were out on strike, maybe the only one to take place while I was old enough to notice, when he did something that I helped with a little bit, which still reminds me that a person can disapprove of the decisions of others but still act for their benefit. Shortly before Christmas he asked someone in the mining camp to tell him who had children for whom there would be no Christmas gifts or special foods. He then gathered up whatever candy, fruit, goodies, toys, just that would serve as special for the children and we drove to those houses where he left the presents on their front porches. I was with him and I saw this myself. He thought the men mistaken to go out on strike but he did what he could for them. He was a good man and I respect his memory.

Daddy was also very funny, very witty, and a great fan of Mark Twain's writing. My dad had the same kind of dry humor as Twain's.

He and my uncle, Papa played tricks on each other and were close friends, living in the same house. They were brothers-in-law because their wives were sisters and we all lived together in a three generational house, 1241 16th Way SW, for about thirteen years until 1953 when my little nuclear family of mom, dad, and three siblings finally moved away from there into our own house three blocks away at 1418 16th Place SW. While we all lived together in the same house, Daddy and Papa shared a lot of their time and had developed a real love for each other. Most of our holiday events were spent with my grandmother and the families of her four adult children, Frank, Phil, Alvice, and Mary Frances. One such holiday meal we were all together at Phil's house waiting on my dad to return from the Blue-Gray football game in Montgomery. We were all seated at the dining room table when Daddy arrived and quickly sat down at the table. Papa started laughing before anyone could see why, but as soon as Daddy picked up his fork it collapsed. Then he held his water glass only to see what looked like a dead bee in it. Papa had gotten all kinds of trick items to put at Daddy's place as a joke.

They really like each other's company, fishing and hunting together during the season, bringing home the squirrels that they had killed. I would sit with them on the floor of the enclosed back porch and watch as they laid out the still-warm bodies of their game to be skinned so that the women could cook the squirrels for our dinner. I watched and had no squeamish dislike for it, taking all in and observing how it was done. Watching the men prepare squirrels for cooking was sort of like watching my mother and aunt when they would kill and scald the chickens raised in our backyard. These were old practices that women and men raised in a rural life knew how to do and were skilled in the doing. We also got fresh unpasteurized milk in the fall when the state fair was held at the fairground in Five Points West. I learned how to churn that milk and make butter from it.

They hunted and both had squirrel guns, which were .22 semi-automatic rifles, and a couple of shotguns each. My dad started teaching me to shoot the .22 before I was really old enough or strong enough to hold it up by myself, so he would prop the barrel in the crotch of a sapling and tell me how to use the sight and aim and pull the trigger. He was adamant on gun safety, telling me to assume that every weapon I saw was loaded and to never point a gun at anything unless I meant to kill it. When we were done with our target practice, he was very careful to kneel and clear the rifle of bullets, showing me how every time. He said the same thing to me every time, "this gun is loaded until you remove the bullets. It is always loaded until you unload it." I grew up knowing there were hunting rifles, shotguns, in our house but what I didn't know was Papa had a hand gun which he usually kept in his store. One night he brought it home and left it on the top of the chest of drawers in the bedroom where he and Sissy slept. I was not supposed to be in there, but kids do a lot of what they are not supposed to do and I saw the gun. I asked Daddy what it was and from the look on his face I knew I was in trouble without knowing why, just knew the look. What he said, perhaps 70 years ago remains with me even now: "that is a gun meant to kill people. It has no other use. Do not touch it ever." The distinction he made was clear to me, young as I was, and I never saw it again. My sister Jane and brother Eddie and I grew up knowing about guns, about what they were for, about how to use them, and with respect for their power.

I fished with my dad and uncle more than I hunted with them. They liked to seine for minnows in a creek to use as bait in the lake they fished most often. The kind of bucket they used to keep the minnows alive is still in use now, I have seen them for sale in some of the older hardware stores. The bucket has two parts, one fits inside the other and is perforated so when the person fishing wants a minnow for bait, she can pull up the inner bucket, the water drains into the outer bucket leaving the minnows flopping around out of water and easy to grab. I don't remember being so much interested in catching fish as wanting to go wherever Daddy and Papa went. I loved being outside with them, minnow seining, walking in the woods while the dogs got to run a while, taking in the lessons my dad was teaching about how to read my surroundings, knowing the best time to hunt in the fall was just after a rain and the leaves were wet and would not rustle. He showed me how to rub the ridged edges of two quarters together to draw the squirrels' attention. It was also when he would take time to point out where an old relative once lived or where the Oxmoor furnace stood before Wilson's Raiders destroyed it during the Civil War. He had spent his childhood on Shades Mountain and his adult life working on both Shades and Red Mountain, so he knew the land. Sometimes we went out to the woods with the dog but carried no guns and did no hunting. I was an excellent shot and loved everything about the process until I killed my first animal; it was the last one. I loved the hunting but not the killing. After that first one I shot tin cans and old bottles only, but I knew where all his old-time people had once lived and worked.

I think that the men in the family might have used their male bonding time to have a few sips, or many sips, of bourbon because there was sometimes an undercurrent of tension when they came home from being out together. I think my mother might have disliked it and while no one said so aloud, kids can pick up the energy without knowing what the facts are. I know that Daddy and Papa would stop by a local tavern, The Little Aristocrat, which was close to Papa's store in West End. I know they stopped in to have a beer together because they took me and my sister in with them, sat us up on a bar stool, bought us each a soda and chips while they had their beer. I usually wanted an Upper-10, or 7 Up and Jane loved Cokes, so we got to pick what we wanted and sit with the men in the tavern. I wonder if our mother ever knew we were there. If she did, she did not criticize her husband in front of us. My mother was in love with him until the day she died, and there was never another man for her from the time she first met him at sixteen.

When they first met, my father still lived in the same house with his mother Rhoda Jane Curl Lemley. When they married, his mother was no longer living and but Daddy's brother Bill and his wife, who I knew as Olene, were living there. As my mother told it, she and Daddy moved into the old family home but my mother did not want to live with her sister-in-law so they moved out. She was always rather sparse in the details of why she did not want to live there, only indicating that she didn't get along well with Olene. Another hole in the story, but that reluctance to tell the details reflected something that she said to me many, many times in the course of my life once I married and had to learn to contend with the newly added family; there can be no arguments or fights within a family between its members. She was adamant on that. She was so adamant that I came to feel very alone in my inability to fit in with my young husband's family once we had two small boys of our own and I did not like his father's style of parenting or grandparenting – my sons. When I complained about it, my mother dismissed my point of view with that annoying admonition that there could be no arguments or fights in the family. One of her favorite sayings was that "blood is thicker than water" when she wanted to explain why family always sticks together, and yet she must have seen me as now belonging to the family of my husband and it was time to think of myself within that relationship: she was mistaken, I was a Lemley.

There was just one problem with that, I didn't know what that meant because I did not know who they were or where they had come from to get to Jefferson County. I had no idea when the first Lemley, or Curl, had entered Jones Valley and settled on its blood red soil. But I have learned that Jones Valley and Red Mountain and the Lemleys and Curls are blood and bone together. We have a family history shaped by the landscape of central Alabama, of Jefferson, Shelby, and Bibb and the rich coal and iron ore seams of those places. Generations of men of the Curl and Lemley families were miners and black smiths and workers in the extractive and productive fields of taking coal and iron from the earth and helping turn it into usable products. Sometimes I imagine that my bones are made of limestone and my blood is red with dust of the iron ore. My memories of that mountain are still vivid scenes of the slag pour off as it ran flowing, glowing, and throwing off sparks from the immense heat. My sense of place, of what grounded me was shaped in such events as watching the white-hot slag rushing out of Spaulding Furnace, of ranging the hills of Shades Mountain with my dad, and later as a teenager driving my sister's little green Chevy coup to watch the white-hot pigs of iron as they were rolled out of the blast furnace at Ensley. Growing up on the disappearing edge of that industry left its' mark on me and I will always feel the tug of those memories, those experiences of seeing the raw materials being turned into useful things thorough the sheer work of men who mined, forged, poured, and hauled the ore. Many of them were descendants of some of my ancestors who came into the valley and climbed up the mountain, sweating and laboring to make a life, men and women who had little in life other than desire and awareness that what they would have derived only from what they could earn from hard, hard labors.

I knew more about my Howell and Philips ancestors, that they had a very different life in Alabama after they moved from Virginia and North Carolina to take their chances farming and growing cotton in the flat, black soil of Perry County. They were not a part of the coal and iron ore saga of Birmingham but of the old agricultural society that was slowly dying out as the new industrial one was being built. I knew about them because they visited us in town and at our house and told the stories that connected me to the past if only by hearing some names so many times that I never have forgotten them. There was a significant difference in how I related to my mother's family and my father's family; I knew the living members of her family and heard the stories of their ancestors, but I knew almost nothing of my father's family other than his four living brothers and their wives and children. I failed to ask him for information while he was living and after his death in 1966 it was too late for his first-hand knowledge, so I had to seek it from other sources. I knew so little about his family that as an adult when I traveled to a city away from Birmingham, and especially outside of Alabama, I would look in the local telephone directory for the name: Lemley, seldom finding even a single one. I wondered if the name had been changed or if the first immigrants entered the country far from Jefferson County and only a few traveled so far south. I wondered where they originated, was the name derived from the English Lumley? At some point in this decades-long search I noticed the name Laemmle and started looking for that version as well. There was one Laemmle, Carl, who was an early member of the nascent film industry and had established movie theatres to show his films, but I never located a connection with him, only that the name continued to pop up from time to time. I wondered but learned almost nothing until living in Germany in the 1970s (about a decade after my father's death) revealed that spelling Laemmle was typical of Bavaria but even that did not produce much so after one more failed effort to track down some clues about the family name, I stopped seeking.

That one failed attempt from the time in Germany happened while I was at work in the Keller Theatre when a young African American soldier came into the theatre in uniform. He was in uniform and the name tag which was sewn onto his shirt was Lemley, so I asked him about his home and where he was from. When he told me Madison County, Alabama I was surprised and excited but he must have found my questions annoying because he left rather quickly, not returning later to talk to me as he said he would. In 1977 it was not a good idea for a Black enlisted man to spend time alone with a White officer's wife – not a good idea for his welfare and I was too lacking in wisdom to know how to handle what should have been a simple exchange, a simple conversation between two adults. However, it did remind me that there had to be some more folks named Lemley in Alabama other than my father and uncles, so I went back to work building the set without ever learning then any more of the Lemleys of Madison

County. I did find them many years later. I did locate some Madison County kin in 2017, but that story has to wait.

My work while in Germany was in the Music and Theatre branch of what was called Special Services (or Recreation Services), meaning the offices and activities which were established specifically to offer special activities for active duty military men and women for the times they were free of work or training, Such activities are still available in bowling alleys, do-it-yourself auto repair shops, photography labs, libraries, and a variety of activities such as the one where I worked, the music and theatre office. For a couple of decades around the era of the war in Vietnam the music and theatre venues were very active and widespread wherever a military base large enough to support a theatre existed. One base in North Carolina,

Fort Bragg, operated three on-base theatre venues in the dinner theatre, a small studio theatre, and the large playhouse which had been converted to a live theatre stage from its original function as a movie theatre. I think it was built during WWII. The operation of such facilities required a staff of theatre and music personnel to mount and stage theatre productions several times a year. I worked for the Music and Theatre in Giessen, Germany. The M&T had a two-fold mission: to provide recreation in the theatre opportunities for military personnel, their families, and civilians working for the US government and to send music and theatre shows out to remote sites for the entertainment for the soldiers assigned to the sites. The theatre I worked in, Keller Theatre, had once been a bowling alley before it was converted into a live theatre space in 1958. As cramped space that it was, it lasted until 2009 when it was closed.

I mentioned that I had more recently, about two years ago, located the Lemley name in Madison County just by typing in the name to see what might come on through Google's search engine. This came after I had used Ancestry.com's DNA test kit and gotten the results back. With the results of the test and a much more advanced computer technology than I had ever had before, I started my internet search for all the branches of my family tree. I had assumed that genealogical data for the Philips line would be the easiest to locate since I have a copy of a book self-published by Henry Poellnitz Johnston in which he had located that particular branch, the Philips, of his own family. However, that was not how it was revealed to me.

His book, *Pioneers in their Own Rights* provided some factual data for me, but after about four generations of that family, the line disappears from the documents. As I have learned since starting this research, the Philips are my "disappearing" branch while the information on the Howells, Lemleys, and Curls is abundant and now I want to trace as much for you, whoever is reading this, of the history and the stories of the Lemleys as I feel confident is accurate. Only with the ease of discovery provided now through the internet have I finally learned enough to satisfy my life-long curiosity. And what I learned was not romantic, no hidden reveals about some character who was well known in the world and I got to discover we were kin!! No, what came a big surprise for me was that I cared so much to have just found their names, to have literally discovered their existences in the flat, one-dimensional form of paper records. As I looked more and more into the past as recorded in census, birth and death and marriage records a strong sense of belonging to a place and having a history overwhelmed me and it felt right to know their names. The desire to be connected to them surprised me. Faulkner had it right when he said that the past was not dead, it was not even past.

My early desire to know about my father's family burned at a high intensity: the desire to locate, to name long dead strangers who are connected to me only in the most accidental way of generations of births and deaths has lately lessened and sits at a much lower simmer. I can recount what I have learned. We all have come from families of some dimension, some rooted and some restlessly nomadic, some large and some as small as a mother and child, but still come from other persons bound to each by biology or choice or spirit but bound nonetheless. The story that has enthralled me began with the departure of the ship The Duke of Wirtenburg, left Rotterdam on 20 October, 1752, bound for Philadelphia. According to the ship manifest, its' commander was Daniel Montpelier. On the passenger list were two names that connect me to that ship: Johanes Lemle and Michael Lomle (with an umlaut on the o). The ship was only one of hundreds which left the area of the Palatinate, now a part of modern Germany. The exodus out of the Palatine was often one of escape for religious reasons, to leave an oppressive atmosphere in the interminable strife among various Protestant denominations and between Protestants and Roman Catholics. The source for this information comes from *Pennsylvania German Pioneers: A Publication of the Original Lists of Arrivals in the Port of Philadelphia from 1727 to 1808.* (ed. Ralph Beaver Strassburger & William John Hinke, published for the Pennsylvania German Society: 1934; Vol. 1, Pages 497-499.

In all genealogical accounts of the Lemley families deriving from Johanes, it is assumed by those researching the family history that he and Michael were brothers. When I write these ideas and findings and suppositions about the Lemley family, I am uncomfortable with the uncertainty. I am accustomed to offering only what I have good evidence to support, or saying, as I did above, "it is assumed" that one man was brother of another, but genealogical research seems to rest on such possibilities, rather than certain documentation. DNA evidence can prove limited information about WHICH Lemley brother was my forebear, but that has to be enough to satisfy my curiosity about when and where the Lemley kin to me entered colonial north America.

I have had an extraordinary life, extraordinary in my own way of thinking what that means rather than by external values. I live in large part in my own mind, an interior life where I think, wanting to connect as many of the seemingly separate and disparate pieces into a pattern that I recognize. I have heard of and read about so many strong images and they have stayed with me, but lacking connections, floating below the surface of my consciousness, being forgotten until a sudden spark breaks open the dark cave of memory and brings these pieces into the light, into awareness, into connection and the perfect patter emerges. I see so much that way, with rapid recognition of exactly where the pieces fit together and what it means to me – to know what I am seeing now for the first time in wholeness, much as T.S. Elliot wrote in *Little Giddens* when he said:

> *Is not redeemed from time, for history is a pattern*
> *Of timeless moments. So, while the light fails*
> *On a winter's afternoon, in a secluded chapel*
> *History is now and England.*

> *With the drawing of this Love and the voice of this Calling*

We shall not cease from exploration
And the end of all our exploring
Will be to arrive where we started
And know the place for the first time.

Poetry saves me. William Shakespeare saves me from tongueless death of silence.

Mary Oliver saves me from being blind to the natural world around me. Hank Williams saves me from forgetting my past and my roots. The poets speak with experiential knowledge that comes from living wide open to all possibilities.

When those separate and sunken bits and pieces are suddenly and unexpectedly brought into union and meaning and into the light, I think myself most richly blessed with my extraordinary life of the mind – because I suddenly know. I see. Ich kenn.

AFTERWORD

Memory has a claim, a demand to be believed, sometimes with scant evidence other than what it tells me happened, or was said. Have you ever returned to place that is still alive in memory only to see that place with new eyes? Or, rather older eyes? I think we walk around in our life without questioning much about it until some part of that life shifts, or ends, or transforms in such a significant way that attention must be paid. Moving from the only house where I had lived until age 10 with my parents, my sister and brother, my aunt and uncle and my grandmother was the first shock to my smooth and unexamined life. I had lived in a world where Saturday had its routine, Sunday had a routine, every Summer was spent as every summer had been spent, and I had an no reason to wonder what might change. I knew the reality of each room, every season, every person's place in my and I was comfortable and safe.

Then my world seemed to tilt on its axis, everything flew off and had to settle back to a steady routine. We moved. We moved 4 blocks away and into a new world. I have moved about 30 times since then, and each time there were shocks and aftershocks, and rearranging both my exterior material life and my interior emotional life as well. And now I can understand the result of this moving, this upheaval in all that is secure and routine, is that I am aware of the past in a different way. I want to say that as a kid everything is as it is because it is all you know, no memory of another time, no reaching back for a forgotten time, life just is. Age ends that. Age nudges, then pushes me to, remember, analyze, question, and there are too many pieces that have now gone missing. There are holes, vacancies in my memories. I want to say that now memory is like the narrator in Our Town who can stand back at a distance and view the past but sometimes cannot call the right actor to show up, can no longer call the actors by name.

Love in the Time of Cholera is a book written by Gabriel Garcia Marquez, and has not much to do with life in the time of Corona virus 19, yet that title continues to course through my consciousness, calling my attention to what we are witness to now, life in the time of a pandemic. For me, little has changed other than to restrict my wandering, to keep us at home and away from our intended trailer travels. But those are minor losses, nothing when compared to what others face daily.

I want to record these days and am having trouble pulling apart the strands of my days, separating the volunteer time in Dripping Springs NM, my physical ailment that made me fear it was cancer in my abdomen, and the multi-pronged reality of the COVID-19. Life right now is still much as I would have it be, quiet and settled with the crowds absent and the beach (supposedly) empty, and I have so many good books to read, yet I drift about, unable to focus or accomplish anything.

LIFE THROUGH MEMORIES

A few weeks ago, as I was editing the fall issue of *Alabama Heritage* magazine, I received a phone call from a man asking for advice about a manuscript he'd found among his wife's possessions after she passed. Mac Montgomery was a stranger to me, but after a short time on the phone with him, I felt a connection with him and his wife's story. Though coping with his loss, the manuscript he'd found seemed to present an opportunity to help his wife live through her words, and those words are an opportunity for all of us to connect not only to Carol but also to the past.

I spend my days reading through many dry history books, but the best stories are the personal ones. Carol Lemley Montgomery's manuscript of her childhood memories growing up in Birmingham, Alabama, during the 1940s and 1950s allow insight into a world that no longer exists. Scenes of multi-family households making ends meet after the Depression; encounters with mining communities and the corporations that structured nearly every aspect of their lives; a rural style of life in what would eventually become a metropolitan area—all of these experiences breathe life into Carol's narrative. But the stories also provide an often unseen and compelling first-hand account of one woman's life in Alabama before the civil rights and women's rights movements took hold of the nation.

Memoirs are strange things—stuck somewhere between fact and imagination. But they bring to life a person's history in a way that statistical documents and dry history books cannot. Carol says it best, perhaps, in her own words: "Our memories are the life blood that runs through our family generation to generation, from my mother, and my father and those who came before." Carol's experiences made her who she was, and her written memories will transfer a bit of her into each one of us.

Susan E. Reynolds, Ph.D.
Editor, *Alabama Heritage*

A LIFE DEDICATED TO EQUALITY, EDUCATION, AND EMPOWERMENT

In a world brimming with remarkable individuals, it's not every day that one encounters a person who leaves an indelible mark on those fortunate enough to cross paths with them. Dr. Carol Montgomery was undoubtedly one such individual, a multifaceted personality whose life was a tapestry woven with threads of compassion, intellect, and a burning desire for justice.

I first came to know of her through her posthumously published work, *Charity Signs for Herself*, and glimpses of her life, were shared through her social media presence. Reading her memoir essay, was like experiencing the joy of capturing fireflies on a calm, Summer evening. I found myself genuinely curious about this incredible woman - who was she, what adventures did she embark upon, and what moved her to laughter or tears?

The Essence of Carol Montgomery

Carol Montgomery was a formidable and highly intelligent woman who carried with her a profound commitment to equity, fairness, and goodness. Her conversations flowed effortlessly from spirited political debates to advocating for women's rights, and even dissecting the nuances of restaurant cuisine. Beloved by many, she was not confined to a single role; she was a pilot, an avid volunteer, a travel enthusiast, and an ambassador for all who aspired to lead better lives. But perhaps her most enduring passion was her unwavering belief in the accessibility and lifelong value of education.

A Distinguished Educator

As an avid historian and educator, Carol Montgomery's impact extended far beyond the walls of academia. She dedicated her life to enlightening and inspiring generations of students. Her teaching career took her to various institutions. Her classrooms were spaces where the quest for knowledge was nurtured, and her dedication to her students was unwavering.

Champion of the Environment

Carol's love for the environment was another facet of her character that shone brightly. She was a passionate advocate for preserving and protecting nature. Her volunteer efforts in coastal North Carolina and her multiple tours at the Department of Interior recreation and refuge sites in New Mexico exemplified her commitment to environmental conservation. Her experiences in these areas fueled her desire for research and learning, a thirst she tirelessly quenched throughout her life.

"*Charity Signs for Herself*"

One of Carol Montgomery's most notable contributions to the world of academia was her groundbreaking work, *Charity Signs for Herself*. This historical masterpiece delves into the lives of female slaves and emancipation in the mid-1800s. Through meticulous research and an empathetic lens, Carol shed light on the struggles and triumphs of these women, giving a voice to those long relegated to the margins of history. Her book continues to serve as a beacon of enlightenment, a testament to her enduring legacy.

A Life Remembered

Tragically, Carol Montgomery's remarkable journey came to an end in 2022. Her passing left a void that cannot be filled, but her spirit lives on through the countless lives she touched, the minds she enlightened, and the causes she championed.

In Dr. Carol Montgomery, we find a woman whose life was a testament to the power of education, the importance of environmental stewardship, and the unwavering commitment to justice and equality. Her legacy continues to inspire us to strive for a better world, one where knowledge, compassion, and dedication prevail. As we reflect upon her life, we are reminded that even in the darkest of times, there are individuals like Carol who shine as beacons of hope and change.

Ana Yousuf-Starns, Ph.D.
Interim Director, *CaryPress International Books*

ABOUT THE AUTHOR

Carol Montgomery was a strong and highly intelligent woman who carried with her a deep sense of equity, fairness, and goodness. She was at home arguing about politics, women's rights, as well as the taste of food at a particular restaurant. Beloved by many, she was a pilot, avid volunteer, travel enthusiast, and an ambassador for all who sought a better life. Carol deeply believed in the accessibility and lifetime value of education.

Born in Birmingham Alabama, She completed her undergraduate work at Armstrong State University in Savannah and her MA and Ph.D. studies at the University of California, Irvine. As an avid historian and educator, she taught at UC Irvine, St John's University (NY), Methodist University, Fayetteville State University, UNC Pembroke, and NC Community Colleges.

Her love of the environment led her to volunteer in coastal NC and multiple tours at the Department of Interior recreation and refuge sites in New Mexico. Carol always loved research and learning; her studies were published in, *Charity Signs for Herself,* a history of female slaves and emancipation in the mid 1800's. Carol died in 2022 and is survived by her husband Mac and three grown children, Paul, Rhoda, and Mary, and their families.